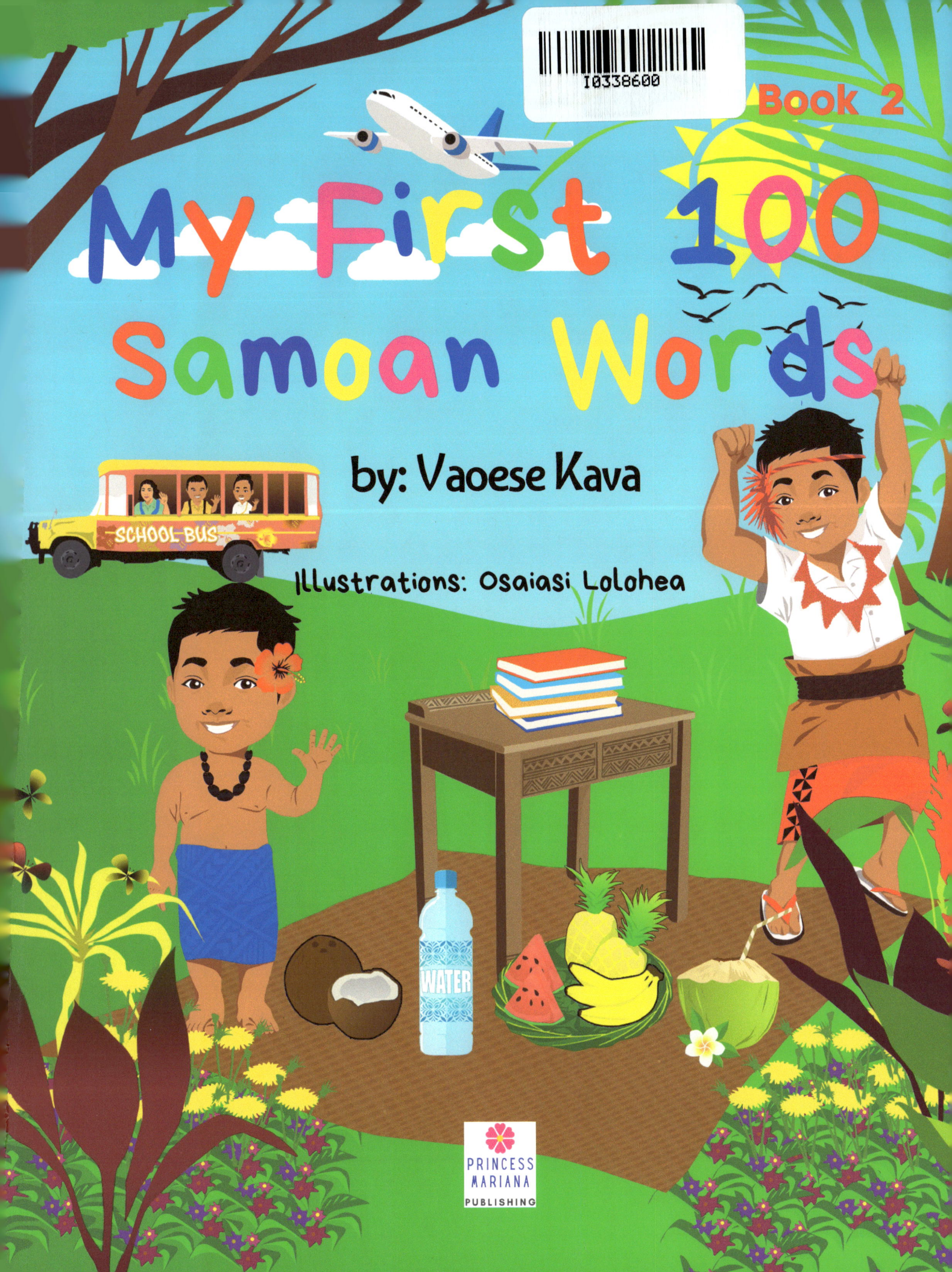

*Dedicated to Makai Malosi
Our Quiet Little Warrior,
Your Story Continues to Inspire*

My First 100 Samoan Words - Book 2
(presented in Basic Phrases in Samoan & English)
Copyright © 2020 by: Princess Mariana
All rights reserved. No part of this book may be reproduced in any manner whatsoever without written permission of the author and publisher. Except in the case of brief quotations and reviews. Thank you for your support and for buying an authorised edition. For more information, pls.
Contact: #VaoeseLimutauKava :
on Facebook & Instagram
Written By: Vaoese Kava
Illustrations By: Osaiasi Lolohea
ISBN 978-0-6450030-2-4 (hardcover)
ISBN 978-0-6450030-5-5 (paperback)
ISBN 978-0-6450030-3-1 (eBook)
Distributed Worldwide
First Edition Nov. 2020

Ua matou fia Ti'etie 'i se Pasi
'i le asō, ma T.J. ma Ellya

T.J., Ellya, and I, would
like to Ride a Bus today

E fai la'u 'Ula Heilala pe'a ou Siva Tonga,
E fa'aali lo'u fiafia 'i le Puna 'i Luga

I wear my Heilala Garland when I do my Tongan dance. I Jump Up when I'm excited

O le Fatatusi lea e tu'u
uma ai a'u Tusi 'e Faitau

This is my Bookcase, where I
keep all my Books to Read

Fa'afetai Tama mo le Laulau ma le Nofoa

Thank you Daddy for my Table and Chair

O le Ta'avale a o'u Matua e Lanu Moana
O le 'a alu tina e fai le Fa'atau

My Parents old Car is Blue,
Mother will drive it to do Shopping

E Lelei tele le Vai mo 'Oe ma A'u

Water is very good for You and Me

E lelei fo'i le inu o le Niu

Drinking Coconut water is also good

'E ese le manaia o Mea'ai na kuka 'e Tina

Mother cooked some yummy Food

Oute Fiafia 'e tafao 'i le Paka i Apia

I'm Happy when I visit the Park in Apia

O le 'a Malaga T.J. 'i le Va'alele.
Tōfā Soifua T.J. Ia manuia lau malaga

T.J. will Travel by Airplane.
Good Bye T.J. Safe Travels

About the Author:

Vaoese Kava "aka" Ese Limutau Noa Aiono has always had a passion for writing since she was a young girl. This later inspired her to complete her Arts and Business Administration studies and earning her MBA from the Australian Institute of Business, South Australia. She's a wife, a mother, and grandmother to the adorable Amulek. Her desire to teach her grandson Samoan led to the completion of this four-book series of a Child's first 100+ basic words & phrases in Samoan & English. She hopes that this book series will encourage parents and child to not only learn to speak Samoan but practice fun and healthy family lifestyle habits. Follow her on Instagram & Facebook #VaoeseLimutauKava

PRINCESS MARIANA
PUBLISHING

I Love You